INTRODUCTION

The Galaxy S24 Ultra is a hell of a phone. As always, Samsung has jammed it full of more high-end hardware than you can shake a S Pen at, and this year it's also packed with cutting-edge AI features. But it's expensive, and most of my favorite things about it have very little to do with the AI parts, which aren't even exclusive to the Ultra

It comes with a display that's so easy to use outside in bright light that I want every other manufacturer to copy it. Its camera system is one of the best in the game and comes with a fantastic portrait mode. The built-in stylus remains one of the nicest and fanciest ways to make a grocery list

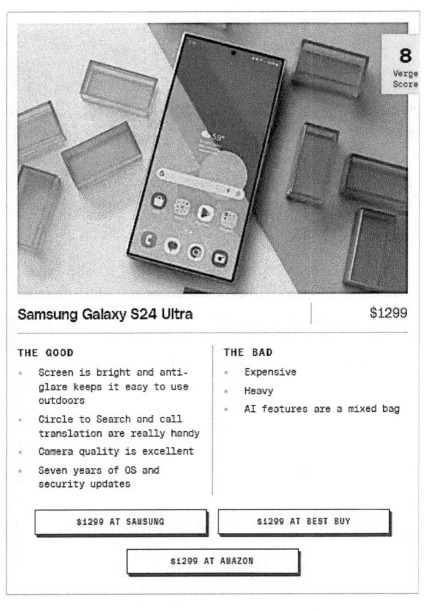

8
Verge
Score

Samsung Galaxy S24 Ultra $1299

THE GOOD

- Screen is bright and anti-glare keeps it easy to use outdoors
- Circle to Search and call translation are really handy
- Camera quality is excellent
- Seven years of OS and security updates

THE BAD

- Expensive
- Heavy
- AI features are a mixed bag

$1299 AT SAMSUNG

$1299 AT BEST BUY

$1299 AT AMAZON

Some of the AI features really are impressive; live translation for phone calls could be really helpful for someone who makes a lot of calls in an unfamiliar language. Voice recording summaries are surprisingly good and give my beloved Pixel Recorder a real run for its money. And turning any video into slow motion is just plain fun. Are the results always great? No, but they're usually delightful. But battery performance is just okay, and while I appreciate the new flat-screen design, it leaves some sharp corners that can be uncomfortable in your hand. Above all, the Ultra is expensive — now starting at $1,299, a $100 increase from last year's model. Samsung's everything-but-the-kitchen-sink device is still the most feature-packed phone money can buy, but I'm just not seeing an extra $100 worth of improvements, especially considering that the AI features will all be ported to the S23 series in a future software update.

CHAPTER ONE

GETTING TO KNOW YOUR SAMSUNG GALAXY S24 ULTRA

The Unpacking Galaxy S24 Ultra

The most recent Galaxy S24 phones were unveiled by Samsung at its January Unpacked presentation. A number of improvements have been made to Samsung's flagship phone over the past year, the Galaxy S24 Ultra. What makes it stand out from the S23 Ultra, and is it a worthwhile upgrade? Probably not, but let me explain anyway.

What we need to do first is examine the alterations. Starting at $1,300, the S24 Ultra is more costly than its predecessor, the S23 Ultra, which was released at $1,200 (and probably cheaper today), but it offers a handful of enhancements over the S23, most notably in the engine department.

The S24 Ultra looks and feels almost identical to its predecessor, down to the rear camera arrangement. Subtle differences exist. For instance, compared to the aluminium S23 Ultra, the titanium frame of Samsung's newest premium phone ought to offer superior durability.

By forgoing the rounded display borders of the S23 Ultra in favour of a flat front, Samsung boldly asserted that the S24 Ultra had 47% less bezel on the sides. With a maximum brightness of 2,600 nits, the new screen is more comprehensible in bright sunlight than the S23 Ultra's 1,750 nits. The most recent and long-lasting Gorilla Glass Armour and Gorilla Glass Victus 2 materials from Corning, respectively, shield the screens of the S24 Ultra and S23.

So, it appears to be identical to the previous generation, with the possible exception of a brighter screen and increased durability. Gaming and other performance-intensive jobs will remain within reasonable limits thanks to the S24 Ultra's cooling system, which features a two-layer thermal insulation and a twice-large vapour chamber.

To recap, the S24 Ultra's cameras are almost unchanged from the S23 Ultra's, with the exception of a 50-megapixel telephoto lens replacing the 10x optical sensor. The new camera may have a shorter optical length than the 10x optical camera on the S23, but its higher megapixel count should make the photos it captures look much clearer. (We will definitely know when we are able to evaluate the two phones' camera capabilities side by side.) The

S24 Ultra gets a 10x optical length thanks to its 5x optical camera and crop zoom.

Compared to the S23 Ultra, the S24 Ultra's Snapdragon 8 Gen 3 processor is noticeably more powerful. Not only does the new premium phone eliminate the 8GB RAM option, but it also restricts customers to 12GB RAM and 256GB, 512GB, or 1TB storage, further streamlining possibilities. The only real change to the hardware is an upgraded processor, which should lead to somewhat better battery efficiency on the S24 Ultra.

With the debut of the S24 Ultra, the new phones' generative AI capabilities, dubbed Galaxy AI, serve as the primary point of differentiation. Circle to Search stands out because it lets you search for anything you've circled on your screen without ever leaving the app you're now using. All it takes is a finger or stylus trace to accomplish this. Finding a certain spot in a friend's vacation photos or identifying an individual's clothing could be two examples of information searches that could benefit from this.

In case you were wondering, the S24 Ultra, like the rest of the S24 series, comes with extra generative AI capabilities including in-call translation and note summarization. Furthermore, it has the capability to suggest different text tones depending on the identity of the receiver, such as a more formal tone for superiors and a more casual tone for friends. Generative AI picture tricks allow users to rectify image tilts and gaps, magnify photos beyond their original proportions, and modify and remove sections from images.

Some generative AI tasks, like live translation, can be executed locally, while others require queries to be sent to the cloud. To ensure the privacy of your inquiries and phone number on the S24 Ultra, you can enable the feature that allows the device to conduct generative AI queries in the settings.

And the worst thing? Galaxy AI will soon be available for certain older Samsung phones, such the S23 series. Eventually, the S23 Ultra will incorporate these capabilities, even if Samsung hasn't announced a release date just yet.

Even without generative AI, the S24 Ultra is an improvement over its predecessor. It helps with things like taking better photos in low light and maintaining image stability when moving. The S Pen attachment is almost unchanged from last year.

Samsung has also increased the amount of time that it will continue to service its most recent phones, which is another significant development. The S24 Ultra will receive seven years of software and security upgrades, including Android 14, out of the box, which is an increase from four years on the S23 Ultra (which featured Android 13). This is a really noteworthy change. Thanks to its increased use of recycled materials—including cobalt in the battery and rare earth elements in the speakers—the S24 Ultra is better for the environment.

Would S23 Ultra Owners Be Better Off Upgrading To The New S24 Ultra?

There are no noticeable hardware upgrades or changes to user experience with the new S24 Ultra when compared to the S23 Ultra from last year. If generative AI or a seven-year battery life are available, then current users of Samsung's premium phones from 2023 will have a solid reason to consider upgrading to the new model.

There have been rumours that the S23 Ultra will eventually include all of the Galaxy AI capabilities. It is unclear when last year's premium phone will be upgraded to support the S24 Ultra's generative AI features, and our main concern is that it will not be able to handle all of them.

The first smartphone chipset to incorporate generative artificial intelligence (AI) into its silicon was the Snapdragon 8 Gen 3 that Qualcomm unveiled in October of last year. Presumably, the new phone's generative AI features are dependent on the same chipset as the S24 Ultra's. Even though it wasn't ready when the S23 Ultra's Snapdragon 8 Gen 2 chipset was announced in late 2022, the processor is capable of running on-device generative AI. On the other hand, for S23 Ultra cloud operations, additional Galaxy AI functions will be required.

The primary consideration for moving up from the S23 Ultra to the brand new S24 Ultra should be the need for generative AI. Please be aware that we are unable to comment on Galaxy AI's merits at this time because to our lack of first-hand experience with the technology. Once our in-depth review of the S24 Ultra is published, we will have a clearer idea of whether it provides an enhanced experience compared to its predecessor. We recommend waiting for the moment if you aren't interested in becoming the first to market with cutting-edge mobile technologies.

The Samsung Galaxy S24, S24 Plus, and S24 Ultra are about to drop, and you better be ready to be amazed. These 2024 smartphones will, in our opinion, be the best of their kind, including cutting-edge hardware and an abundance of premium features. But if you get your hands on one of these devices, you better make sure you have all the extras you need to really make it shine.

A new phone cover isn't the only accessory for the Galaxy S24 that you might consider purchasing. To maximise your purchase, you can choose from a variety of accessories, such as wireless charging stands, power banks, headphones, and smartwatches.

It is for this reason that we have compiled a list of the Galaxy S24 accessories that we think work best with the device. Whether you're into working out, listening to music, or simply wanting your phone to last all day, we have something for you. Presented here are some of the best add-ons for your Samsung Galaxy S24.

Superb battery life drawbacks compatible with SmartThings and rated IP67 Pricey Color options are limited $30 on Amazon $30 LG Electronics This Bluetooth tracker is an improved update to the original GalaxyTag, allowing you to more easily tag and monitor your possessions. It has a long runtime of up to 500 days on a single charge and is water and dust-resistant (IP67). You can use it in conjunction with Samsung's SmartThings Find system. Its user-friendly monitoring experience allows you to monitor your beloved stuff from the convenience of your hand. Our top pick for a Galaxy S24 item tracker $30 on Amazon I am reviewing the Samsung Galaxy Buds 2 Pro. 1 Photo by Phil Nickinson / TED Talks The 2 Pro Samsung Galaxy Buds Optimal headphones for the Samsung Galaxy S24 The 2 Pro Wireless Earbuds from Samsung Superb comfort and fit Lots of useful functions Their appearance is superb. A respectable amount of time between charges for "360 Audio" is subpar Poor head tracking $70 on Amazon ABT Electronics $180 $269, Walgreens Get a pair of Galaxy Buds 2 Pro if you're a die-hard Samsung fan. In addition to a high-definition chat experience and a fully immersive 360-degree audio experience, these earbuds provide an Intelligent Active Noise Cancellation feature. These headphones are available in a rainbow of hues and, with the case that comes with them, have a talk time of up to 29 hours. The actual buds have a maximum runtime of eight hours when ANC is turned off and five hours when it is turned on. This is the one pair of earphones you should get for your Galaxy S24. The 2 Pro Samsung Galaxy Buds The 2 Pro Samsung Galaxy Buds Optimal headphones for the Samsung Galaxy S24 $180 AMAZON Related Top sales on the Samsung Galaxy S22: Major discounts on unlocked versions Here are thirteen of our favorite cases for the Samsung Galaxy S24 Plus in 2024. In 2024, these are the top 15 covers for the Samsung Galaxy S24. Review of the Samsung Galaxy Watch 6 15. Digital Trends contributor Joe Maring Seiko Galaxy Watch 6 Our top pick for a Galaxy S24 smartwatch Pros and Cons of the Samsung Galaxy Watch 6 Excellently cozy style Exciting and vibrant show Adorable are smaller bezels. Samsung The health situation is improving. Dependable, high-quality results Extended runtime on a single charge Remains an excellent buy CONS Wear OS is far from perfect. A little more costly $400 LG Electronics If you own a Galaxy S24 series smartphone, you'll love the Samsung Galaxy Watch 6, which has many functions for monitoring your health, exercise, and overall well-being. Everyone, regardless of their lifestyle or budget, may find the ideal smartwatch among the many available models and pricing points. While Samsung's state-of-the-art fitness tracking capabilities keep you on top of your exercises and help you reach your objectives, the built-in sleep coach helps you monitor your sleep patterns and obtain better rest. Plus, we tested the battery life and found that it may last up to two days, so you can go about your day without worrying about losing power. Our top pick for a Galaxy S24 smartwatch Samsung 400 Third-generation Oura rings reviewed on the finger Digital Trends' Andy Boxall The Oura Ring is the top smart ring compatible with the Galaxy S24. Advantages of the Third Generation Oura Ring • Elegant style • Effortless and cozy • Educative and user-friendly software • Precision in monitoring sleep • Longevity of wearable batteries • Streamlined charging process • App access requires a subscription. Not a single fitness metric Not everyone can get by without a wristwatch. $299 Usa, Inc. The Oura Ring is one of the most talked-about wearable tech products of the past few years. Its extensive feature set is almost indistinguishable from that of modern smartwatches. This gadget gives you a complete picture of your health and wellness by analyzing your sleep patterns and activity levels. Plus, you may pick a size and style of Oura Ring that perfectly complements your own unique style. This is the one to get till the Samsung Galaxy Ring is released. The Oura Ring is the top smart ring compatible with the Galaxy S24. Advantages of the Third Generation Oura Ring • Elegant style • Effortless and cozy • Educative and user-friendly software • Precision in monitoring sleep • Longevity of wearable batteries • Streamlined charging process App access requires a subscription. Not a single fitness metric Not everyone can get by without a wristwatch. $299 Usa,

Inc. The Oura Ring is one of the most talked-about wearable tech products of the past few years. Its extensive feature set is almost indistinguishable from that of modern smartwatches. This gadget gives you a complete picture of your health and wellness by analyzing your sleep patterns and activity levels. Plus, you may pick a size and style of Oura Ring that perfectly complements your own unique style. This is the one to get till the Samsung Galaxy Ring is released.

THE NEW WALL CHARGER IS IDEAL FOR THE GALAXY S24

• Quick charging • Contains three USB-C devices • The charging power is 67 watts. On the more expensive end of the spectrum Amazon ($45) The fast-charging technology in this Belkin wall charger allows it to charge your phone up to 50% in as little as 23 minutes. It is perfect for charging MacBooks and other USB-C laptops because it can supply up to 67 watts of electricity over a single connector. If you own an iPhone, Galaxy S24, tablet, or any other device that requires rapid charging, this charger is the way to go. It features three USB-C connections, each of which can access 25W, 20W, and 20W, respectively. It is a really practical accessory to have because it is small and can be taken with you wherever. If you own an iPhone 15 Series, MacBook Pro, AirPods, Galaxy, or any other device that supports rapid charging via USB-C, then you need the white Belkin BoostCharge 3-Port USB-C Wall Charger with PPS 67W. Wall Charger with Three USB-C Ports by Belkin BoostCharge An optimal wall charger compatible with the Galaxy S24 Amazon ($45) Digital Trends contributor Christine Romero-Chan Micro Power Bank by Anker An ideal battery pack for the Galaxy S24 POSITIVES • Little imprint • Environmentally friendly • Several color options •

Conveniently features a screen It can be too small for certain people. $ 50 ANKER Any person who is always moving around will benefit greatly from this portable charger from Anker. It is available in a variety of hues, allowing you to select one that complements your individual style. The built-in USB-C connection makes charging your Galaxy S24 a breeze with this power bank. You won't have to worry about running out of juice for your phone as often thanks to the 10,000mAh battery. Considered environmentally friendly, this power bank is a top pick. Its 80 percent recycled plastic content lessens its negative effect on the environment and helps cut down on carbon emissions. We recommend this to the majority of S24 users, although power users might wish to seek out a bigger choice elsewhere.

An optimal battery pack for the Galaxy S24

TANKER $100 Mophie Universal Wireless Charging Stand.

An Air-Charging Station for Your Mophie Muffy

The Galaxy S24 has a premium wireless charger.

Sure to be compatible with any mobile device that can use Qi wireless charging Stylish and contemporary Made by a trustworthy manufacturer Just fifteen watts of power. With Mophie's Universal Wireless Charging Stand, you can charge your

Galaxy S24 and any other Qi-enabled smartphone. The 15W power output makes it compatible with many Qi-enabled phones, such as those from Samsung, Apple, Google, and others. It stands out because it can charge even in the thinnest of smartphone cases (up to 3 mm). Charging in either portrait or landscape mode means you can use your phone even while it's charging.

THE MOST EFFICIENT WIRELESS CHARGER FOR THE GALAXY S24

Introducing the Belkin PowerCharge Pro Flex.

Abelkin Adaptable Professional BoostCharge by Belkin An Adapter for USB-C

The best USB-C cable for the Galaxy S24

The perfect accessory for any USB-C device

It's a bit pricy compared to other USB-C cables, but it's resistant to more than 30,000 twists and has a very long length.

This USB-C cable is compatible with a wide range of devices, one of which is the Galaxy S24. Its construction was able to withstand over 30,000 twists because to the use of ultra-flexible silicone technology. For this reason, your USB-C charging cable will serve you well for many years to come. With it, you can easily charge, sync, and connect all of your devices. Nothing else noteworthy has occurred. This cable for USB-C is excellent!

If you own a MacBook Pro, iPad Pro, iPhone 15 Series, Galaxy S23, or S22, or any other USB-C device, you need this black Belkin BoostCharge Pro Flex Braided USB-C to USB-C cable to charge it effortlessly and swiftly. Additionally, USB-IF has certified it.

Superior BoostCharge USB-C Pro Flex Cable from Belkin

The perfect USB-C cable for the Samsung S24 Loyal Consumers

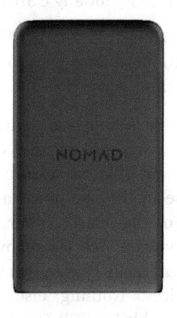

AN ULTRA-THIN 35W NOMAD POWER ADAPTER

One of the most effective thin power adapters for the galaxy s24 pros 35W of power packed into an ultra-thin GaN device

Downsides: Nomad is up there with the best of them.

One USB-C connector $30 NOMAD GIFTS

Look no further than the 35W Slim Power Adapter if you're in search of a charging solution that saves space. Built with GaN technology, it quickly charges your Galaxy S24 and other devices with up to 35W of power. This charger's ultra-thin profile makes it ideal for use in any setting, whether at home or on the move. This pickup is perfect for frequent flyers and other travellers because it has one of the slimmest charging ports available.

35W of power packed into an ultra-thin GaN device

Downsides: Nomad is up there with the best of them.

Nomad Goods $35 for a single USB-C port

Look no further than the 35W Slim Power Adapter if you're in search of a charging solution that saves space. Built with GaN technology, it quickly charges your Galaxy S24 and other devices with up to 35W of power. This charger's ultra-thin profile makes it ideal for use in any setting, whether at home or on the move. This pickup is perfect for frequent flyers and other travellers because it has one of the slimmest charging ports available.

A Thin Power Adaptor That Works Well With The Galaxy S24

Loyal Customers $35 HyperX Chargeplay Base wireless Qi charger.

This is the HyperX Chargeplay Base.

The best-selling Galaxy S24 portable charger: • Easy to use with two devices at once • Works with any Qi-enabled gadget • More expensive than competing options **£39 at ASOS**

The HyperX Chargeplay Base is an excellent choice for anyone in search of a wireless charging solution for their electronic gadgets. This charging pad supports several devices at once, so you can charge your Galaxy S24 and other devices, like wireless headphones, all at once.

With the Chargeplay Base's rubberized cushions, you can charge your devices without worrying about them falling off. You can easily keep track of your devices' charging status with the LED charging indicators. Qi certification also means that the Chargeplay Base has went through all the necessary safety and performance inspections.

THE NEW SAMSUNG GALAXY 24 ULTRA CHARGING AND BATTERY

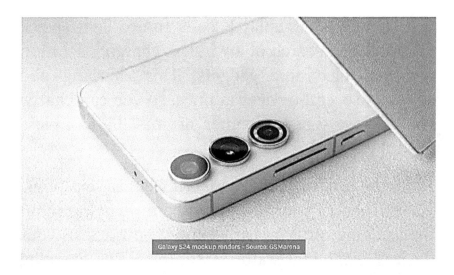
Galaxy S24 mockup renders - Source: GSMarena

When it comes to technology, the Samsung Galaxy S24 series is making waves. For a while now, it has been circulating. 3C has now officially certified three of these devices in China. We can get down to the nitty-gritty now.

MODELS OF THE SAMSUNG GALAXY S24 TESTED TO HAVE OUTSTANDING CHARGING TIMES

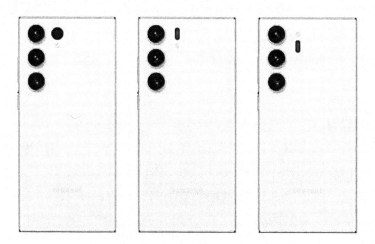

An example of a Samsung Galaxy S24 model is the SM-S9210. The following one is the Samsung Galaxy S24+, with the model number SM-S9260. All devices are capped off with the Samsung Galaxy S24 Ultra (SM-S9280). Who exactly is causing such a stir? The primary consideration is the charge rate.

The scoop is that when comparing the charging speeds of the S24 and S23 series, there isn't much of a difference. The S24 will keep the charging speed at 25W. The S24+ and S24 Ultra, meanwhile, are prepared to revolutionise charging with their 45W capabilities. This crucial information originally came from the certification.

Prior to this one's disclosure, there were other reports circulating. There were hints about the battery capacity of the S24+ and S24 Ultra dropped by a Korean regulatory agency, ELENTEC India, Ningde New Energy of China, and Samsung SDI Vietnam.

A little larger 4900mAh battery, as opposed to the 4700mAh battery seen on the S23+, is supposedly going to be featured on the S24+. Similar to the S23 Ultra, the S24 Ultra might retain its robust 5000mAh battery.

Word on the street is that the standard S24 might feature a bigger battery—maybe even 4000mAh—rather than the 3900mAh seen in the S23. But so far, no official certification has confirmed this detail.

Finally, with minor improvements to battery capacity, the charging remains a priority in the Samsung Galaxy S24 series. We will eagerly await additional official announcements so that we can monitor the performance of these devices in the ever-changing smartphone market.

SAMSUNG GALAXY S24 SERIES BATTERY LIFE AND CHARGING TIMES IN RELATION TO OTHER PHONE MODELS

Samsung's Galaxy S24 series of smartphones offers large batteries and fast charging capabilities. For instance, the iPhone 14 Pro Max has a 27W charging capability, whereas the Google Pixel 7 Pro has a 30W charging capability. Other high-end smartphones with faster charging speeds include the OnePlus 11 Pro (80W charging) and the Xiaomi 12 Pro (120W charging).

Battery life of the Galaxy S24+ and S24 Ultra is exceptional when compared to other premium smartphones. Compared to other top-tier smartphones, such as the iPhone 14 Pro Max (4323mAh) and the Google Pixel 7 Pro (5003mAh), the Galaxy S24's battery capacity might be lesser.

Also, if you're using OneUI 6 and the Galaxy Camera, you might find these tips and tricks from Samsung useful.

Charging times and overall battery capacity are not particularly impressive on the Galaxy S24 series. However, when compared to other brands' flagship smartphones, they manage to hold their own.

Discover a table that pits the Galaxy S24 series against other top-tier smartphones in terms of charging times and battery capacities:

Gizchina Updates Every Week

 For all your needs related to smartphone charging, join GizChina on Telegram! Strontium-24, 25-inch, 4000 mAh macrometer Galaxy Ultra 45 from Samsung Pixel 2 XL 27.4323 from Samsung 14-inch iPhone Pro

Of the 30, 503 Android One, Pixel 7 Pro

The Xiaomi 12 Pro ranges in price from 120,000 to 46,000.

Cost: 5,000 85 OnePlus 11 Pro

The Galaxy S24 series ranks about average when looking at battery capacity and charging time. Your mileage may differ from these estimates of possible capacities and speeds.

HOW TO TURN OFF YOUR SAMSUNG GALAXY S24 ULTRA COMPLETELY

Has the correct method of powering down your Samsung Galaxy S24 Ultra eluded you? No need to stress; here are three simple methods to turn off your device. Use the power button, speak commands, or access quick settings—we've got you covered. Shall we dive into the meat of the matter?

The Three-Step Process for Turning Off Your Samsung Galaxy S24 Ultra

The First Strategy: Using the Panel for Quick Settings

If you like things done simply, you'll love the Quick Settings Panel. This is how it's done:

Two-finger swipes from the top of the screen will bring up the Quick Settings menu.

To access the menu, press the Power icon, which is located in the upper right corner next to the Settings symbol.

hover over "power off."

Once more, press "Power off" to validate your choice.

Option 2: Hitting the Power Button

If you'd rather use the time-tested way of hitting the power button, here you go:

• Wait for the Power button on your Samsung Galaxy S24 Ultra to blink before releasing your finger from its grip.

• The Power menu will appear on your screen.

Pick "Power off." after that.

• Press "Power off" again to confirm your selection.

Thirdly, using Bixby

With a touch of futuristic interaction, Bixby is the ideal companion for voice commands:

• Press and hold the Power button for a brief period to activate Bixby.

For Bixby to turn off while it's not in use, simply say "Power off."

• Bixby will immediately power down your phone upon your command.

Here are some more things to keep in mind when using your Samsung Galaxy S24 Ultra:

With the Power menu, select "Restart" to turn the device back on.

To change how your power button works, go to Settings > Advanced features > Side key.

To restart your Samsung Galaxy S24 Ultra, press and hold the Power and Volume Down buttons for 10 seconds in the event that it freezes up and stops responding.

More information regarding the price of the Samsung Galaxy S24 Ultra S Pen may be found here.

Finally, you won't have to waste time trying to figure out how to turn off your Samsung Galaxy S24 Ultra. Bixby, the Power button, or the Quick Settings Panel allow you to choose the method that suits you most. Powering down your device has never been easier than by following these simple steps. With this newfound information, you can confidently power down your Samsung Galaxy S24 Ultra.

CHAPTER TWO

HOW TO SET UP YOUR SAMSUNG GALAXY S24 ULTRA USING FAST PAIR

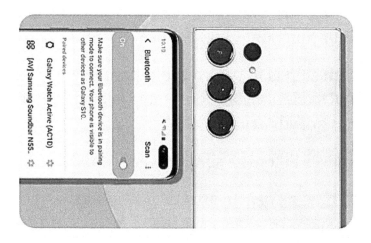

The new Samsung Galaxy S24 is incredibly easy to set up using Android's Fast Pair feature. Pairing Bluetooth devices, such earphones andsmartwatches, is another feature of this service. THE GALAXY S24'S FAST PAIR SETUP PROCESS

Get the new Galaxy S24 up and running. First Stage.

Second, set up your old device close to your new one. It ought to be compatible with nearly any phone running Android 10 or later.

Third, activate the Wi-Fi and Bluetooth on your old smartphone.

Fourth, a notification saying "Set up Galaxy S24" will appear on your prior device. You can call this a Fast Pair function. Click on the "Set up" option.

The fifth step is to use your old phone's QR scanner. If a QR code appears on your Galaxy S24 screen, you can quickly scan it.

Choose Wi-Fi for the sixth stage.

Step7: Use the deactivated device's PIN.

Step 8: Press You have the option to use a QR code or install an eSIM.

As a ninth step, you can tap on Next or Don't copy.

Putting Smart Switch on your old phone—if it wasn't a Galaxy—is the ninth step. Follow the on-screen instructions precisely.

Step Eleven: On the S24's Smart Switch screen, touch Allow.

Twelveth Step: Choose a Transfer Method: Wired or Wireless.

In Step 13, your phone will start searching for available data. Pick one of these choices to move forward with the transfer: All, Only calls, Contacts and messages, or Personalise.

Step 14: Press the Accept button on the privacy screen for Google Services.

Choose a Search Engine as the Fifth Step.

Make a decision about installing Google Assistant in Step 16.

Level 17. On the Advanced Intelligence information screen, click Next to proceed.

Procedure 18. Step 19 is when you get to pick the display mode—light or dark—that suits you best.

Twenty. Please click the Finish button.

HOW TO GET A SAMSUNG ACCOUNT AND ENJOY THE ADVANTAGES OF HAVING IT

A Samsung account is a free membership service that allows you access to all of Samsung's features across all of your devices. Stay with us as we walk you through the process of creating a Samsung account.

Please ensure that you are using the most current software version for your device before trying any of the methods given below. To update your mobile device's software, follow these steps.

1. Head over to Settings and then choose Software update.

2. Step 2: Get the software and set it up.

3. Following all on-screen instructions is the last step in Step 3.

ADVANTAGES OF HAVING A SAMSUNG ACCOUNT

All sorts of devices, from smartphones and tablets to computers and TVs, may access Samsung services when you sign up for a free Samsung account. Many Samsung services may be accessed using a single Samsung account, saving you the trouble of signing up for each one separately. Premium apps like SmartThings and Samsung Pay are available to you with your Samsung account, along with other perks like data backup, recovery, and syncing across devices. If you ever forget your password, this will come in handy.

First, you can sign up for an account by going to the Settings page.

Any Galaxy phone or tablet you buy will come with the Samsung account software already installed.

Choose Accounts and backup from the Settings menu to begin.

Secondly, before adding an account, locate the Accounts option and click on it. Lastly, sign up for a Samsung account.

Third, either enter your login information or click the "Create account" button to make an account from scratch.

The fourth step is to click the "Agree" button once you have read the legal materials.

Fifth, when you're ready, hit the "Create account" button.

LEARN HOW TO HANDLE YOUR SAMSUNG ACCOUNT.

When you create an account with Samsung, you'll have the choice to sync your accounts or utilise the newly-introduced 2-step verification feature to make your account even more secure. To access the

Samsung account you created, just follow these steps.

Go to the main menu and select Settings. Next, go to Accounts and select Backup.

Next, head over to the Accounts section.

Step three: Pick the Samsung account you've previously created.

Verifying Dual Authentication: The Gold Standard

Go to the main menu and select Settings. Next, go to Accounts and select Backup.

Step 2: Next, locate the registered Samsung account and tap on it in the Accounts section.

Third, locate the Security option and select Two-factor authentication.

Ways to personalise Samsung's apps and services

To begin, navigate to Settings > Accounts to see the backup option.

Step 2: Next, locate the registered Samsung account and tap on it in the Accounts section.

Thirdly, pick Samsung apps from the Apps and Services menu.

Be aware that your wifi provider, software version, and device may alter the available options and displays.

if your Samsung phone, tablet, or wearable is acting strangely, you may report it via the Samsung Members app. eliminate that part of the text At this point, we can look at the present scenario with more precision. We only keep the anonymized data for the duration of the study. If you're having trouble with the Samsung Members app, here's how to report it: Using the app: the essentials.

HOW TO TRANSFER DATA TO A NEW SAMSUNG GALAXY PHONE VIA WI-FI, USB-C OR PC

The long-awaited Samsung Galaxy S24 phones are either already available at your neighbourhood store or will be available very soon, depending on the time of day you read this. Regardless, you've landed on this page because you want to know everything there is to know about moving data to a brand new Samsung Galaxy phone, S24 or any other model.

You should be aware that your new Samsung Galaxy phone supports three different methods of data transfer: Wi-Fi, a USB-C cable, and your computer. The catch is that you'll need Android 4.3 or later on both devices to use any of these three methods—Samsung's own Smart Switch software.

Those of you who are currently using an iPhone and are interested in moving your data to an Android device can find detailed instructions on our dedicated tutorial page. Another one of our guides is for moving information from an Android device to an iPhone. The procedures for copying data from an older Android device to a new Samsung Galaxy phone are described in the sections that follow.

Needs And Equipment

- Two smartphones—one of them is a Samsung—running Android 4.3 or later.

- Samsung Smart Switch software • A stable wireless network • A USB-C cable, if desired • A computer with Windows 7 or later installed, if desired

MOVE YOUR DATA TO A NEW SAMSUNG GALAXY IN A MINUTE

Launch the Smart Switch app on both devices and follow the on-screen instructions to complete the Wi-Fi data transfer.

To transfer data via USB-C, connect the two devices using a USB-C cable. Then, open the Smart Switch app on both devices and follow the on-screen instructions.

Data transfer is as easy as connecting your old device to your computer with a suitable cable and installing Smart Switch on your PC. The data from your previous phone can be easily transferred to your new phone by first transferring it to your computer. Instead of picking Backup this time, go with Restore.

Procedures for Transferring Data Through Wi-Fi

To begin, activate the Smart Switch on each gadget.

Using Smart Switch over Wi-Fi is the most hassle-free way to transfer all of your data, including contacts, photos, and music, to a new Samsung phone. Just almost every new Samsung phone has the Smart Switch app—look for it in the Settings or Search menu. If your current device isn't a Galaxy, you'll need to download Smart Switch from the Google Play Store in order to transfer data. This download requires an Android device running 4.3 or later and at least 1.5 GB of storage space.

Two, fire up the Smart Switch app on each of your mobile devices.

Prior to using either device, ensure that the Smart Switch app is installed. For first-time users of Smart Switch, acceptance of the terms and conditions is required. Press Allow on the screen asking for permission to move on to the Transfer step.

The next step is to set up wireless networking between the two devices.

Just make sure the two devices are connected to the same Wi-Fi network before you proceed to link them. On the previous phone, go to the Send data menu and select Wireless. To access the Receive data option on your new Galaxy phone, press Galaxy/Android, followed by Wireless.

4. Sync data across many devices

Select the amount of data to transfer on your old phone before pressing Allow. To begin the migration, click the Next button. The amount of time remaining will be shown by a percentage graphic. Pick Return to Home from the drop-down menu.

A GUIDE TO USING A USB-C CABLE FOR DATA TRANSFER

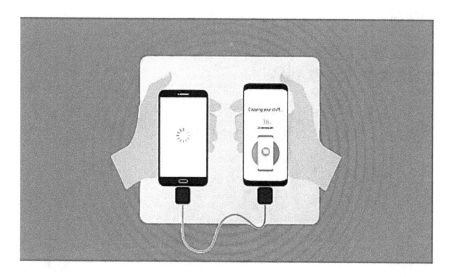

1. Use the USB-C cable to link the two devices.

To transmit data via a USB-C cable, you need to launch the Smart Switch app on both **devices. To**

summarize, follow steps 1 and 2 above. Next, use the USB-C cable that came with your Samsung phone to link the two devices.

2. Share information across various gadgets

To enable backup on your brand-new Samsung phone, open the Smart Switch app and go to the Backup menu. To begin the migration, choose the quantity of data you wish to transfer, and then touch Start. To show how much time is left, a % graphic will be displayed. After that, choose Return to Home.

STEPS FOR USING A COMPUTER TO TRANSFER DATA

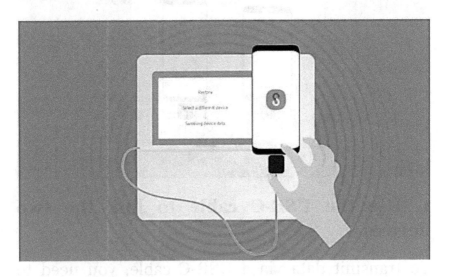

1. Get a Smart Switch installed on your computer.

Before you may transfer data using a PC, make sure that the PC has Smart Switch installed and that it is running Windows 7 or later.

Second, hook up your outdated gadget to your computer.

After that, use a cable that is compatible with your PC to link your outdated device to it.

3. Transfer all of your old phone's info to your computer.

Next, go to the Smart Switch interface on your PC and choose Backup. Then, on your old phone, tap Allow to start the transfer procedure. After finishing, press OK to end the call.

Connect the new gadget to your computer. 4.

You should now use a cable that is compatible with your computer to link your new device to it.

5. Move all of your files to the new gadget.

Press the Restore button on your computer's Smart Switch interface. Tap on Samsung device data, followed by Select a different backup. Here is where the data transfer can start.

CHAPTER THREE

WHAT IS NEW IN YOUR SAMSUNG GALAXY S24 ULTRA

How To Use The Magic Editor On Your Samsung Galaxy S24 Ultra

The Pixel 8's Magic Editor is only one of its many remarkable features.

Your support is crucial to Android Police. If you buy something after clicking on one of our links, we might get a small commission. Find out more details.

Magic Editor, a groundbreaking AI tool that anybody can use to edit photographs with only a few taps, was released with the Google Pixel 8 and Pixel 8 Pro. This tool is powerful and can significantly alter your photographs, despite its apparent ease of use.

To help you get the most of Magic Editor, we have included comprehensive tutorials, real-world examples of its possibilities, and useful advice. After you give the Pixel 8 a go, you should investigate all of its interesting features.

In What Ways Is Magic Editor Versatile?

Magic Editor simplifies editing by automating complex operations with artificial intelligence. These approaches will be recognisable to anyone who has used Photoshop or any other programme for editing images.

With Magic Editor, you can: • Snap a photo and extract its elements.

Purge your life of items you no longer want.

Change the arrangement

Change the sky by making clouds appear or disappear.

Include a sunset.

Use special effects to make it stand out.

Of course, not every shot will have a perfect effect in every possible way. For example, the sunset effect is not applicable to inside shots. In the same way that the Apple logo in this image refused to budge no matter how hard we tried to select it, complex things aren't always easy to edit.

If you want to know what Magic Editor is capable of, the best thing to do is to get your hands on it.

Getting Started with Magic Editor

To start using Magic Editor, you'll need a Pixel 8 or Pixel 8 Pro, as well as a reliable internet connection. Despite having access to advanced AI capabilities through the Tensor G3 chip, Magic Editor processes images in the cloud using Google Photos.

Make sure you save a copy to Google Photos before you use Magic Editor to edit your photos. You are now free to commence after attending to this matter.

Magic Editor: Starting Up the Programme

1. Open Google Photos and find an old picture to see.
2. You may locate the Magic Editor button in the screen's lower left corner. Press on it.
3. Tap on an item to choose it.
4. As soon as you touch an object, the Magic Editor tools that are relevant to that image will be shown.

5. When you're done editing in Magic Editor, use the Save copy button on the right side of the screen to save your changes.

Relocating and resizing images

This tool is perfect for situations where your subject is partially out of frame or when something is obscuring your vision. Magic Editor does its best to fill in the object's pertinent details and background.

All you have to do to use this tool is choose an item and then drag it with your finger. You may also pinch it to make it smaller or larger.

dog-friendly flat with a beige carpet

Use this tool sparingly and only for simple, easily-located things. Below is an image of a complex item that was selected, which prompted Magic Editor to fill the empty spaces with bizarre, alien-looking objects.

Factor n the Impact of the Weather or Sunsets

You may change the appearance of the light and weather by taking a picture with the sky in the background. This Magic Editor programme has always worked reliably for me.

Storm clouds are placed on the bottom picture, while the upper picture shows the Golden Hour effect.

Remove Any Obstaclesi

Now available on all smartphones through Google Photos, Magic Eraser was offered by Google with the Pixel 6's release. A more refined variant of this feature is available on the Pixel 8 and Pixel 8 Pro.

To erase an item's touch, press the erase button.

Using Magic Editor, you can achieve a lot more. What matters most is the quality of the image you take. Try out different photos to find the one that works.

ADVICE ON HOW TO MAXIMIZE MAGIC EDITOR'S POTENTIAL

While not perfect, Magic Editor is a powerful programme. Follow these guidelines to keep yourself out of trouble.

Magic Editor isn't the best choice for panoramas or photos that are still in the editing process.

After modifying an image in Google Photo using one of the other tools, be careful to save and reopen the file. Use of Magic Editor will be enabled thereafter.

The Magic Editor's pop-up window shows the panoramic image mistake.

Make sure you swipe through for the best results.

By utilising an editing tool, Magic Editor produces a multitude of versions. Hit the "right" button to select the one that best suits your tastes.

The following photographs show the different results of removing the object in the first picture using Magic Editor.

When working with complicated photos, Magic Editor often produces a confused outcome, as seen in the samples above.

Make It Possible To Process Edits.

Even with the processing power of the cloud, Magic Editor still takes time and makes your Pixel 8 heated. If your Pixel phone is charging or if it's really hot outside, you should wait for the changes to finish processing before utilising this function

Refrain From Making Unauthorised Changes.

Magic Editor does not allow you to change everything, for reasons that may include Google's GenAI terms or simply practical considerations. These are the things that Magic Editor won't let you change. When you attempt to modify these items, an error message will be displayed.

• Confidential paperwork, including bank data, personal identification documents, and more.

• The anatomy and physiology of a human being.

• Large areas for selecting.

• Images including discernible human subjects.

MAXIMIZE YOUR EDITING POTENTIAL
WITH THE PIXEL 8'S FEATURES.

Not only does the Pixel 8 include Magic Editor, but it also has a plethora of other editing tools. Best Take, an app that lets you swap out faces in group shots for those from similar ones, was another one that caught our eye.

HOW TO MAKE AND USE AI-GENERATIVE WALLPAPERS ON YOUR GALAXY S24

Ways to Make and Use Galaxy S24 AI-Generated Background Images

A family named Gupta

An Abbreviated Form of the Initial

• The Galaxy S24's AI Generative Wallpaper function allows users to create an infinite amount of wallpapers.

To access the feature, locate the Creative section in the wallpaper settings. Pick Generative from the drop-down menu to make custom wallpapers.

• To make your own AI wallpaper, choose a template from Samsung's many choices, edit the text prompts to your liking, and then hit Generate.

After last month's introduction, all eyes were on Samsung's newly revealed Galaxy S24 series and the many artificial intelligence features it included. But if you're a Galaxy S24 owner, you could have missed the AI Generative Wallpaper—a function that allows you to make an endless amount of AI backgrounds.

The regular Galaxy S24 series backgrounds are still accessible, despite the fact that it's an additional feature. So, what's the point? Have you any thoughts?

Benefit from the AI-Generated Background Images on Galaxy S24 Phones

A feature called AI Generative Wallpaper was debuted with the Google Pixel 8 series last year. Now you can find it on Samsung's top-tier devices, and it performs identically to the original.

Therefore, I obtained a standard Galaxy S24 from the Beebom office and tested this feature for you. Take a look at it:

To get the home screen on your Galaxy S24, press and hold for a lengthy period of time.

• Go down the menu until you see the option to alter the background and style.

• Then, choose "Change wallpapers" from the main menu.

• Next, locate the Generative option by scrolling down the Creative panel. To go to this page, click here.

Here at the top, you may find a number of pre-made templates at your disposal. You can choose to join them if you so desire.

Still, pick one of the nine AI Generative templates from the "Create something new" section to activate this feature.

Then, in case you were unaware, NLP takes what you say and turns it into visuals. Because of this, the primary function of this interface will be to edit text. Tap on the sections of the prompt that you wish to modify. Pick the one that works best for you.

• Press the Generate button thereafter. By tapping on a generation you like, you may set it your home screen wallpaper, lock screen wallpaper, or both. Click on the Next button.

You can make as many different versions of an image as you want. You can create up to four distinct image variants with every click of the Generate button.

You can preview wallpapers on this page. In this section, you can find the clock, widgets, and other settings that allow you to customise your lock screen.

• Click the Done button in the upper right corner of your screen when you are through customising. OK, I'm done!

Individual Parts We Have the Thought That You Could Benefit From

How to Turn Text into a Video with These 10 Best AI Video Generators

Arjun Shaul

On June 29, 2023,

In 2024, these are the 8 best picture enhancers powered by AI, both free and paid.

The 30th of January, 2024, Sha Arjun.

15 Best AI Apps (Free and Paid) for Android and iOS

May 3, 2023—Shankara Upanishad

Well, that's all! You can now personalise your Galaxy S24 with an AI-generated wallpaper. The created images are also of respectable quality, making them perfect for use as background images on computers. My favourite artificial intelligence wallpapers for my Galaxy S24 are:

If you like these wallpapers, you may grab the high-resolution versions by clicking this Google Drive link. No need to worry, Galaxy S23 owners! Samsung has assured us that the Galaxy S23 series will soon have the same AI capabilities as the Galaxy S24 series.

Those fortunate enough to possess a Samsung Galaxy S24, S24 Plus, or S24 Ultra can now enjoy the AI wallpaper feature. We expect this capability to be included in the OneUI 6.1 update for the Galaxy S23 series. Furthermore, regardless of whether you own Samsung items or not, these AI art generators can assist you in creating some remarkable wallpapers.

You can use Circle to Search and other fantastic AI capabilities from the Galaxy S24 on your Pixel phone. The linked instructions should give you a good idea of what to expect. Please share your preferred AI wallpapers with our community by posting a comment below now that we've confirmed that.

CHAPTER FOUR

SAMSUNG BIXBY: WHAT IT IS AND HOW TO USE IT

WHAT IS BIXBY?

In the digital assistant market, Samsung has Bixby, which goes up against Siri from Apple and Assistant from Google. Every top-tier Samsung device, including phones, TVs, refrigerators, and more, comes pre-installed with it. In comparison to competing voice assistants, Bixby excels in several areas. Its few drawbacks explain why, after being on the market for over five years, it has failed to gain widespread acceptance. Keep reading to find out everything you need to know about Bixby, including its features, ways it differs, compatible devices, and how to use it.

Quite a bit can be done with Samsung's digital assistant Bixby just by speaking to it. This follows on the heels of S Voice. Bixby can do the usual fare of voice assistants: send texts, check the weather, make calls, launch apps and control music playing.

Unlike Siri and Google Assistant, Bixby can communicate with a wide variety of system settings and even third-party apps. On your Samsung mobile, you can manage the brightness, activate and deactivate auto-rotate, take a picture, and reply to Gmail emails all using your voice.

The other two virtual assistants allow you to do things like chat with friends and family or change the system's default settings. Bixby can see your Instagram DMs and YouTube subscribers, but they can't access anything else. This is the key feature that sets Bixby apart from the competition.

To set up and use Bixby, you must first sign up for or log into your Samsung account.

Bixby can execute a wide variety of simple tasks on the device itself, which is another differentiating factor compared to Google Assistant. This makes the voice assistant capable of carrying out multiple commonplace commands even when no internet connection is available. You must download the Bixby app to your mobile device in order to access this mode.

BIXBY: HOW TO INSTALL AND USE IT

If you own a Samsung smartphone, you can use Bixby. It may be used without any additional software that you can find in the Play Store.

There are multiple ways to launch Bixby on a Samsung phone:

- For a few seconds, press and hold the side key or the Bixby key (if available) to activate Bixby.
- Say "Hi, Bixby." when you meet. You need to enable Bixby on your mobile device for it to work.

- Locate the Bixby shortcut in the app drawer.
- If you are unable to access Bixby using the side button, you can make adjustments by following these procedures.
  1. Access the Settings menu on your Samsung phone.
  2. Navigate to the section about advanced features.
  3. Move the hand to the side.
  4. You may enter the settings by tapping the gear icon that appears next to "Open app" and then selecting the radio option.
  5. Select Bixby from the menu that appears.
  6. You can also select to associate the side key's press-and-hold feature with Bixby.
  7. favoured side keys for Samsung devices

Soon after you launch Bixby on your mobile device, you will be asked to choose a voice from which you will receive responses. To choose a different voice sample, just touch the corresponding radio button and push the Continue button. Make sure that Bixby is granting the appropriate permissions. Click the button that says Continue.

Introducing the Samsung smart assistant—always ready to help you out. Here is how you can instruct it:

- "Record a video."
- "Show me the emails received today."
- "Ask Google Duo to call my wife."
- "Show the files in the document category."
- "Ask Netflix to play Sacred Games."
- "Start a five-kilometer run."
- "Transfer data from my old phone."
- "Make the screen darker."

Bixby autonomous system command list

THE BIXBY VOICE ASSISTANT

Voice, Vision, Commands, and Text Call are the four main features that make up the Bixby experience.

The Name Bixby

Asking this assistant to "Hi, Bixby" is all it takes to start using its voice feature. You need to enable Bixby Voice before you can use the hot word, though. You may teach the virtual assistant to recognise your voice by saying "Hi, Bixby" over and over again. Here are the steps you need to follow to enable Bixby voice wake-up and begin utilising it.

1. Make Bixby available on all of your gadgets.

2 Click the cogwheel symbol.

Wake up with the sound of your voice.

4. Find your Bixby preferences.

5. Start Bixby speaking

Turning the Respond to my voice option on will allow you to teach Bixby to recognise your voice and react accordingly.

To teach the assistant, just say "Bixby" five times as the computer asks.

Bixby allows you to share your voice.

While training, converse with Bixby.

Use the Speak smoothly toggle if you'd rather not to hear a confirmation of your command. You will have full command of the digital assistant once Bixby Voice is set up.

Bixby can still have conversations with you even when it's not activated. You don't need to know the word to command Bixby to do useful things in some scenarios. Saying "Answer phone" or "Reject call" when a call comes in lets you decide whether to take it or not. "Snooze" or "Dismiss alarm" are additional options for pausing or dismissing an alert. Just follow these steps to make it work for you.

The context of the ads

1. As said before, go to the Bixby Settings page.

2. Pick the option to talk to Bixby even when you're not awake.

Turn to the other side.

BIXBY EYE CARE

Samsung provides Bixby Vision as a substitute for Google Lens. By angling the camera in the desired direction, you can focus on an object more closely with this feature. Similarly, Bixby Vision lets you scan an image and then do things like copy text from it, translate languages, identify objects, or read aloud text.

Turn on your Galaxy phone's camera.

2. Select "More" from the menu.

Third, touch the Bixby Vision icon in the upper left corner.

Fourth, by pointing the camera at an object, Bixby Vision may scan it and provide you more details about it.

5. An up-to-the-minute translation is available under the Translate tab.

6. To copy text from photos, press the T key.

7. Use the Discover mode to peruse the product's description and images.

Press the Wine tab in Bixby Vision to see more information about a certain bottle of wine.

Bixby commands, compatible with Samsung's digital assistant, work in a manner analogous to Google Assistant Routines. This function makes it possible to automate certain phone tasks with the press of a single button. Give me the rundown.

Press Learn about Bixby.

1. Select Quick commands from the menu that appears at the top (three dots).

2. Get familiar with the Bixby menu.

3. After reading the instructions, it is recommended that you start anew with a new one.

4. To start, type a brief command or hit the plus sign.

6. Press Adding a command is as easy as selecting the desired action from a compatible app.

6. Insert the directive and phrase from Bixby.

That is all that is required prior to the processes indicated before. Everything is possible here. A number of functions can be accessed by simply saying "Good Morning" to Bixby. These include disabling Do Not Disturb, activating Always on

Display, checking the weather, reading the day's schedule, and much more besides.

BIXBY TEXT CALL

Samsung's take on Google Pixel's call screening is called Bixby Text Call. Originally released in South Korea with the Android 13-based One UI 5 upgrade, Bixby Text Call was later expanded to include English support in One UI 5.1. Its primary function is to screen incoming phone calls.

As the other party speaks, the virtual assistant instantly transcribes their words. The next step is to type in your reply or choose an instant reply. If you get calls all day from random numbers and would rather not waste time answering them, this is a fantastic option to have.

Nearly all Samsung devices running One UI 5.1 have Bixby Text Call available in English. This includes the Samsung Galaxy S23 series.

BIXBY TEXT CALL: HOW TO TURN IT ON

1. Turn on your Samsung Galaxy phone and open the phone app.
2. In the upper right corner, you should see a menu button (three dots). Press it.
3. Select Settings.
4. Select the Bixby messaging option.

5. Turn on the device's toggle switch.
6. "Language and Voice," select Bixby. You can choose between four distinct Bixby voices.
7. The Bixby Text Call's rapid replies can be edited using the rapid replies option.

BASICS OF MAKING A BIXBY TEXT CALL

When a call comes in after you've enabled the feature, you'll have the option to use Bixby Text Call.

1. To start a conversation via text message, tap the Bixby Text Call option when offered.
2. Sliding the incoming call button confirms your choice.
3. The page that displays incoming calls on a Samsung Galaxy phone
4. After hearing a message, Bixby inquires as to the reason behind the call.
5. The voice assistant begins transcribing the caller's remarks the second they start speaking.
6. Bixby will send your personalised message to the caller or you may choose from the offered quick responses.
7. To answer the call, press the voice call button on top. If you don't want others to be able to hear you, your phone will keep the microphone muted.

Make sure you can receive voice calls in order to use Bixby Text Call. You can't use it for video or voice over IP calls.

CHAPTER FIVE

HOW TO KNOW MORE FEATURES OF YOUR SAMSUNG GALAXY S24 VS S24 PLUS VS S24 ULTRA

The S24, S24 Plus, and S24 Ultra are the three ground-breaking smartphones that make up Samsung's Galaxy S24 line, which has become the epitome of innovation. In this comprehensive review, we delve into the realm of AI-powered capabilities that set new standards for the industry while transforming smartphones.

ONE OF THE MOST IMPRESSIVE FEATURES OF THE SAMSUNG GALAXY S24 SERIES

has an optical 5x zoom lens that lets consumers enjoy the highest level of photography possible with the help of AI zoom. With the help of the ProVisual Engine and the Adaptive Pixel Sensor, astounding 100x zoom photos may be captured with absolute clarity.

Chat Assist Makes It Easy to Send Perfectly Timed Messages Misunderstood messages are a thing of the past with Chat Assist. Chat Assist optimises your language usage, making it effortless to type on the

Samsung Keyboard while properly conveying the right tone in your communications.

The Easy Way to Search Your Screen: Circle to Search The new Circle to Search tool from Google is here, and it's revolutionary. You may quickly search the contents of your phone's screen with a long press of the home button. By touching, squiggly-tapping, or circling an object, you can initiate a search without leaving the app.

Generative Edit: Revealing the Mysteries of Picture-Taking If you want your photos to look their best, use the magical Generative Edit feature. It seamlessly blends altered areas and fills in blanks in the backdrop.

Quickly and Easily Slow Down Videos 5. In the event that you forget to enable slow motion before starting to record, Slo-Mo will catch you. Use this feature to insert frames into your video files so you won't miss a thing.

Using Live Translate to Break Down Language Barriers 6. You may overcome language barriers with the help of Live Translate, which offers real-time translation for chats or phone calls. With this state-of-the-art feature, which is compatible with thirteen languages and seventeen dialects, the native phone app is fully functional.

Automated Image Capture at Night See whether Nightography works better for your night photos. Sharpening, noise reduction, and shaking elimination are all made possible by its AI-powered features. Make use of the Dedicated ISP Block for the best noise reduction results.

Introducing Note Assist, the Ultimate S-Pen Helper! Rejoice, all you lucky owners of the Samsung Galaxy S24 Ultra! Note Assist is an excellent tool to use with a S Pen if you wish to organise your notes by section, bullet point, heading, or even just to make them look neater.

Voice transcriptions made easier with transcript assist You may get precise transcriptions of your voice notes as you speak with the built-in Transcript Assist feature of the voice recorder. It even includes paragraph and sentence breaks. An easy-to-use feature for making travel notes.

Comprehensive Evaluations of the Method As we put these state-of-the-art features to the test in the real world, be sure to check back for comprehensive reviews of all the phones. Superb work!

Comprehensive Evaluations of the Path

As we put these state-of-the-art features to the test in the real world, be sure to check back for comprehensive reviews of all the phones.

Comparing Sizes The dimensions of the Samsung Galaxy S24 Compact are 5.79 x 2.78 x 0.30 inches, and it weighs 5.93 ounces.

The somewhat larger Samsung Galaxy S24+ measures 6.24 by 3.00 by 0.30 inches and weighs 6.95 ounces.

The Samsung Galaxy S24 Ultra measures 6.40 by 3.11 by 0.34 inches and weighs 8.22 ounces. Only S Pens are supported.

A Unified Strategy

All of the devices have a curved rectangular form. The S24 Ultra stands out from the curving S24 and S24+ with its square design. Includes the IP68 seal of approval for protection to dust and water.

Showcase a Range of Roles

Includes flat panels with a maximum brightness of 2,600 nits and an adjustable refresh rate of 120 Hz. The S24 has a 6.2-inch screen with Full HD+

resolution. An impressive 6.7-inch QHD+ screen graces the S24+. An S24 Ultra that supports QHD+ and has a 6.8-inch screen.

Performance Proficiency

Utilises a system on a chip developed for Galaxy handsets, the Snapdragon 8 Gen 3. We improved overall performance by upgrading the NPU, CPU, and GPU. Discover the latest AI features offered by Samsung.

Save and Organise Your Data

S24: 8 GB of RAM, 128 GB or 256 GB of storage space to choose from. We increased the memory of the S24+ and S24 Ultra to 12GB. Storage options for the S24+ range from 256 GB to 512 GB. Pick from three different storage capacities with the S24 Ultra: 256GB, 512GB, or 1TB.

First-Rate Networking

All of the devices are 5G ready, thus they can function with the most prominent US carriers. Among the S24 Ultra's added features are Bluetooth 5.3, near-field communication (NFC), and Wi-Fi 7. Connect your S24 or S24+ to Wi-Fi using the latest 6E standard.

Camera innovations S24 and S24+ form a consistent triple-lens system with a 50MP main shooter, a 12MP ultra-wide, and a 10MP telephoto. The ultra-wide 12MP camera is retained in the S24 Ultra, but the primary camera now boasts 200MP along with a 50MP telephoto lens that offers 5x optical zoom. All variants have the same 12-megapixel front-facing camera. Every one of them is capable of recording in 8K at 30 frames per second, but their batteries are different.

Power supply: 4,00 mAh (S24). Added 4,900mAh battery life to the S24+. A battery life of 5,000 milliampere-hours is maintained by the S24 Ultra. It is compatible with wireless charging up to 15W and offers a variety of wired charging speeds.

Knowledge of Software

All of the phones run on Android 14, which is customised with Samsung's One UI 6.1. Updates to the operating system and security patches are guaranteed for seven years. The software's Bixby and Dex features are incorporated.

The Samsung S24: A Shopping Guide

If you prefer to take notes by pen, the S24 Ultra is a great choice because to its large screen and excellent telephoto lens. If you prefer a larger tablet, the S24+ strikes a nice balance between processing speed and battery longevity. The little S24 has all the benefits of the Snapdragon 8 Gen 3 for people who don't require extremely rapid charging.

To sum up,

The Samsung Galaxy S24 series represents a significant advancement in smartphone innovation with its abundance of AI-powered capabilities that redefine user experiences. Both photography and language translation stand to benefit greatly from the next generation of portable electronics.

HOW TO WORK PRODUCTIVITY WITH THE S PEN ON YOUR GALAXY S24 ULTRA

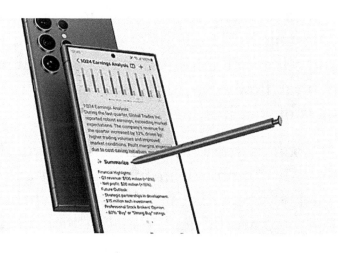

Samsung has made their now-iconic S Pen even more powerful with the release of the Galaxy S24 Ultra. No matter where your job takes you, the S Pen has always been seen as a magical tool that will make your phone more efficient, intuitive, and creative. The S24 Ultra features not only the tried-and-true use cases, but also Galaxy AI, which opens up a world of new capabilities for the S Pen.

The following are seven tips for making the most of the Galaxy S24 Ultra's S Pen:

1. Make a list of things to do and make some notes.

Every business meeting, whether it's with a new client, to launch a massive project, or to hold a monthly staff meeting, requires careful note-taking and documentation of next steps. The Galaxy S24 Ultra's S Pen, when used in conjunction with Samsung Notes, allows you to jot down to-do lists and other vital information in a way that mimics the natural flow of writing, helping you to make the most of your busy day.

As soon as you remove the S Pen from the device, the Air Command menu will appear. You may quickly access the shortcuts and capabilities of S Pen, a powerful and versatile tool for increasing business efficiency, from that location. To make your Notes more comprehensible, you can use images or audio recordings. Any time you choose, from any Galaxy device, you may access and edit your cloud-stored notes.

While you shop, be sure to take advantage of the discount prices.

Find out about the latest deals on state-of-the-art Samsung items.

Look at Sales

Contact a solutions specialist by dialling their number.

For expert advice, talk to a solutions specialist.

Go to a professional

2. CAREFULLY PLAN YOUR NOTES

Time is money in the fast-paced business world of today. Rushing from one meeting or phone conversation to the next leaves little time to do anything more than jot down a few notes. Note Assist, found only on the Galaxy S series and first introduced on the Galaxy S24 Ultra, uses the power of Galaxy AI to automatically translate, format, and summarise any content in your Samsung Notes.

Everything in your Notes is in its rightful place, so you won't have any trouble finding anything. Whether you're taking meeting minutes, making lists, or detailing the next steps, a phone that allows you to take notes simply and freely will keep you occupied. Instead of wasting time sorting through your notes, put that energy towards something more productive.

3. Select and annotate

Additionally, Smart Select may be accessed with a single tap from the Air Command menu. Simply draw a box or lasso around the region you wish to remove from the screen to cut it out. Among other things, you'll be able to annotate and extract text after you've made your selection. You can access a chart where you can express your opinions by tapping on the Smart Select option again. Now you have Smart Select as your best friend for mobile markups.

To search Google, use the circle.

All the essential details are now within easy reach thanks to Galaxy AI and the newly added Circle to Search with Google function on Galaxy S24 Ultra. By drawing circles on your phone's screen, you may quickly find event venues, keynote speakers, and trends. You will see the search results in a new window that opens automatically. Tour the area. Seek out. Get back to work. Dude, it's so simple.

five. Fluent in more than thirty languages

Possessing strong linguistic and idea-sharing skills is essential in today's multicultural and globalised business environment. The Translate option in the Air Command menu is like having your very own personal translator, whether you're conducting business across borders or just working with coworkers in your own country who don't speak the same language. To see the translation in real time, just choose the source and target languages, then mouse over the word or block of text. With the Translate tool, you can quickly translate emails, documents, and even spoken text by tapping the speaker icon. It supports more than 30 languages.

6. Press the lock screen to write.

Explore the Advanced Features option in Settings once you're comfortable with S Pen and Air Command on Galaxy S24 Ultra. The "Screen off memo" and other supplementary features are located here. You can jot down notes on your Galaxy S24 Ultra without ever unlocking the screen if you enable Screen off memo. With zero taps, efficiency is even more crucial than before. To write down a crucial reminder, like a meeting time or due date, just remove the S Pen from its slot. Which phone model would be ideal for your company? GRADUATE TEST Find out which smartphone is most suited to your company's needs by taking this short test. Get It Now

7. Manoeuvre

If you're using certain apps that support Bluetooth, you can use the S Pen as a remote control to get more done. You may access all the available gestures by pressing the button on the side of the pen, which will activate the Air Actions menu. With the S Pen's gesture capabilities in the Camera app, you can easily take selfies to promote your brand on social media, use your phone on a tripod for campaign photo shoots, or start and stop videos. Require more detail? To zoom in, simply circle the S Pen clockwise. To swap cameras, simply swipe up and down. With just the tap of an S-pen, you may effortlessly advance PowerPoint slides during that upcoming important meeting. Must expand? You might want to think about using Samsung DeX on a bigger screen so that your message is seen to everyone.

GET MORE DONE USING

On your phone, you conduct a great deal of business. With the S Pen, you can accomplish even more. S Pen on Galaxy S24 Ultra offers numerous productivity benefits, including a flatter screen for a larger perspective, edge-to-edge S Pen compatibility, and Samsung's brightest display yet. Your multi-function mobile device can also serve as a blank slate for handwritten emails, text-to-handwriting conversion, and ideation. You can't buy a S Pen separately; the Galaxy S24 Ultra already has one built in, making it a formidable new tool in your arsenal. With a Samsung Business Account, you can get a free case and 50% off Samsung Care+ in addition to unique volume pricing, free shipping, and updates on the Galaxy S24 Series. You can also trade in your old phone in bulk and enjoy free shipping.

HERE ARE FIVE WAYS TO USE SAMSUNG'S SMART CHOOSE ON YOUR GALAXY PHONE:

Take screenshots, create GIFs, and extract text from images—all with the help of Samsung's Smart Select function.

Have you ever wished there was an easier method to get the text from a web page or document? The Smart Select tool from Samsung, luckily, is available to assist.

Your Samsung Galaxy smartphone has a cool function called Smart Select. It has a lot of features for recording, editing, and sharing videos. In order for you to fully utilise it, allow me to show you some of its most prominent features.

SAMSUNG GALAXY SMART SELECT ACCESS

You should always have Smart Select on available; it's a fantastic screen capture and selection tool that works well for both personal and business use.

Before you can use the tool, you need to install the Smart Select option and configure the Edge Panels function. Choosing Smart Choose from the Panels menu under Edge Panels is the best option here.

Option for customising the Samsung Galaxy Edge's screen settings

Simply slide in from the edge of the screen to access it whenever you're ready.

To access the advanced editing options in Smart Select, you can use the Air Command features on your Galaxy device that are compatible with the S Pen. You can also download these helpful apps to maximise your use of the S Pen.

1. Screen Capture: Get Pictures And Notes Directly From Your Screen

Smart Select allows you to capture screenshots and save them to your image collection. This programme makes it easy to create and share information on several platforms, including social networking applications.

To use Smart Select to take a screenshot of your screen, follow these steps:

1. Move the cursor to the right or left at the screen's bottom, and then choose Swipe up from the Oval or Rectangular to reach the device's edge panel.
2. Once you've decided on the shape, you may easily crop and resize your image. Simply hold down the tool's corners and drag them to

select the area you want to take a screenshot of. Please press the Finish button.

3. A variety of tools are available in the menu located at the bottom. To save the image to your Gallery, click the downward pointing arrow.

2. Using Text Selection And Ocr To Extract Text From Images

With just a few touches, Smart Select can extract text from photos (such as a business card or a web article), much like other optical character recognition (OCR) applications. It's a handy text-selection tool. Both time and effort can be saved by using this simple tool. Permit me to elaborate:

- Take a look at the side panel of the gadget.
- Pick between an oval and a rectangular shape. When you've picked out the whole thing, you can resize the picture by dragging its edges. You can now selectively extract the text you desire. Please press the Finish button.
- Press the T symbol on the toolbar after the image editor opens.
- There will be a pop-up window that displays the retrieved text. You can choose to remove all of the parts or just the ones you like.
- Select Copy or Share to move the files to another application.

MAKE GIFS WITH YOUR PHONE'S ANIMATION FEATURES

The programme also allows you to capture a short clip from any video playing on your Galaxy smartphone and convert it into a GIF that you can share. The maximum time for a GIF is fifteen seconds, and you have the option to pick between high and standard quality. Permit me to enlighten you:

1. Start by selecting a video to watch. You can utilise YouTube or a URL on your mobile device for this.

2. Select Animation in the resulting side panel, and then to capture a specific part of the screen by dragging the box.

3. Tap the capture button on the screen's bottom to select the scene you wish to capture.

4. At the end, hit the Stop button.

5. After that, you can just hit the down arrow button to save it to the Gallery app.

  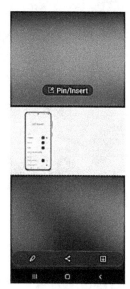

Tools For Annotation: Draw Or Highlight Images Or Text

Smart Select simplifies the process of importing image files and highlighting key parts of an article.

After taking a picture, tap the pencil sign to get a range of annotation options.

The text size and colour can be adjusted to suit your preferences. After making edits and annotations to your images, you can save them to the Gallery by using the Done button.

USE SMART SELECT ANYCONVCOM GIF3-(1)-1 TO DRAW AND ANNOTATE. DIRECT ACCESS: SAVE A SNAPSHOT TO THE HOME SCREEN OF YOUR PHONE

You can quickly and simply save your current location on a map or a specific section of a page to your bookmarks using the Smart Select tool.

This tool allows you to pin pieces of documents, images, or web pages to your home screen so you can quickly access them. Permit me to enlighten you:

1. To select a specific shape for your phone's screenshot, head to Settings > Edge > Rectangular or Oval.

Choose an image, crop it to fit, and then click the "Done" button.

3. Press the Pin/Insert button located at the top of the screen to include a screenshot into your home screen.

The abundance of picture editing tools available makes it easy to add a personal touch to your photographs. You may still edit your photographs to perfection with Smart Select's basic drawing and cropping capabilities. Making a beautiful collage is only one of many things you can do with your edited photos after you've saved them to your gallery.

Combine your Samsung Galaxy Gallery photos with those from AnyConv.com to create a stunning collage.1500 by 1400

S-PEN ACTIONS UNLEASH POWERFUL SMART SELECT FEATURES

You can quickly and simply save your current location on a map or a specific section of a page to your bookmarks using the Smart Select tool.

This tool allows you to pin pieces of documents, images, or web pages to your home screen so you can quickly access them. Permit me to enlighten you:

1. To select a specific shape for your phone's screenshot, head to Settings > Edge > Rectangular or Oval.

2. Choose an image, crop it to fit, and then click the "Done" button.
3. Press the Pin/Insert button located at the top of the screen to include a screenshot into your home screen.

The abundance of picture editing tools available makes it easy to add a personal touch to your photographs. You may still edit your photographs to perfection with Smart Select's basic drawing and cropping capabilities. Making a beautiful collage is only one of many things you can do with your edited photos after you've saved them to your gallery.

Combine your Samsung Galaxy Gallery photos with those from AnyConv.com to create a stunning collage.

CHAPTER SIX

HOW TO ENABLE SWIPE GESTURE NAVIGATION ON YOUR SAMSUNG PHONE

With every new Samsung Galaxy phone, you can be sure that it comes with button navigation. Debuting on Android phones in 2011, the three-button navigation bar is a classic design. A "home" button, a "back" button, and a "recent apps" button comprise the software.

Though it isn't as well-known, Android's swipe gesture mechanism is reminiscent of Apple's iPhone. To access the home screen, swipe up; to see recently used apps, press down the home button; and to go back one page, swipe from the side. You can give these iPhone-inspired motions a go by following these steps:

To start, open the "settings" app and navigate to the "display" option. Scrolling down a bit is required to locate the "navigation bar" section.

On this page, you can see both navigation options side by side. The small bar at the bottom of the screen is called "gesture hint," and if you find it unpleasant, you may disable it.

A "more options" button is also present on this screen. This is the place where you can be really precise. You may customise the swiping style, add another gesture to launch Google Assistant, and adjust the sensitivity of the motions.

And with that, the matter is closed! Try both ways of navigating Android to find out which one suits you best.

I think it's fantastic that both options are available instead of attempting to force one on everyone. Still, it's puzzling that, in 2023, Samsung phones still come preloaded with the antiquated navigation interface.

HOW DO POWER OFF OR RESTART YOUR SAMSUNG GALAXY PHONE

Using the Quick Settings panel or a button combination, you can access the power menu on your Samsung Galaxy phone.

• Press and hold the side button and the volume down button simultaneously to turn off or restart your phone.

• To stop Bixby from being activated when the side button is held, go into the power menu and change the settings.

If you haven't updated your Samsung Galaxy phone for a time, you might be surprised to see that you can power down or restart it by holding down the side button. Are you surprised by that? Bixby is Samsung's virtual assistant. These days, there are a few different ways to go to the power menu on any Samsung phone, be it an S22, S23, or even the latest S24.

Down below, I'll show you how to turn off Bixby entirely and how to enter the power menu using a secret combination of buttons and the Quick Settings app. Alternately, you can tell Bixby to turn off or restart your phone if you mistakenly activate the assistant, saving you the trouble of learning a new method.

We Now Have the S24 Extreme and S24 Plus in Stock!

MENU FOR THE SAMSUNG GALAXY POWERTHE GALAXY PHONE'S QUICK SETTINGS PANEL AND HOW TO USE IT TO TURN OFF THE DEVICE

Through the Quick Settings panel, you may rapidly access the power controls on your phone. Knowing where to look is crucial. If you want to find it, here are the steps:

1. Swiping down from the top of the screen after opening your phone will bring up the Quick Settings menu.

The power button is located at the very top of the screen. Squeeze it.

3. A number of buttons, including Power off, Restart, Emergency call, and Medical info, will show once you do this.

4. Press the icon of an activity to carry it out. Select the icon again when prompted.

YOUR GALAXY PHONE HAS A HIDDEN BUTTON COMBINATION THAT YOU MAY USE TO POWER IT OFF OR RESTART IT.

If you are unable to locate the Quick Settings panel or just cannot find it, you can power down or restart your Galaxy phone using the physical buttons on its side. Instead than just pressing the side button, the new way to start Bixby involves pressing the volume down and side buttons at the same time. It is essential to move slowly because a single press will take a screenshot. I recommend holding on to them until the power menu pops up.

METHODS FOR HARD REBOOTING YOUR

You may turn off or restart your Galaxy phone using the physical buttons on the side if you can't access the Quick Settings panel. The new method to activate Bixby is to simultaneously press the side button and the volume down button, rather than only the side button. Because a single press will capture a snapshot, it is vital to move slowly. Until the power menu appears, you should cling to them.

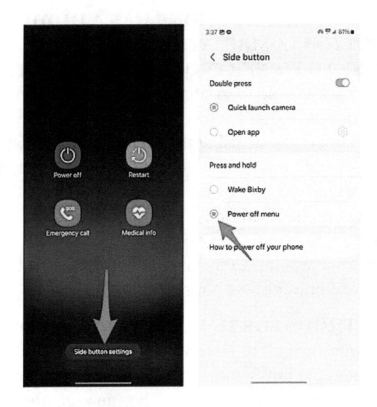

PUT AN END TO ACTIVATING BIXBY WHENEVER YOU PRESS THE SIDE BUTTON

Pressing and holding the side button on a Samsung Galaxy phone will launch Bixby, the digital assistant from Samsung. You can always return to the power settings of your previous Samsung devices if you prefer not to have it:

The power menu can be accessed using the combination of buttons or the quick settings panel, as mentioned above.

Select "Side button settings" from the drop-down menu at the bottom of the page.

Choose "Power off" from the Press and Hold menu to turn off Bixby.

Pressing the side button twice on this screen allows you to customise its behaviour. By default, it launches the camera app. However, it may be configured to start the app of your choice.

CHAPTER EIGHT

HOW TO CUSTOMIZE A SAMSUNG PHONE'S NOTIFICATION SOUNDS

The sound you select to alert you to incoming calls, texts, or social media updates is crucial, as it is the primary indicator of when someone is attempting to get in touch with you. No matter what kind of smartphone you have, from the latest Galaxy S23 to the more affordable Galaxy A53 5G, Android offers a wide variety of settings for the notification sound. WHAT'S ON SECTION Methods for customising the tone of all your alerts The best way to customise app-specific notifications A guide to customising the sound effects on your Samsung phone Methods for disabling Samsung phone-specific alerts The Samsung phone's notification sound snooze feature

DIFFICULTY EASY DURATION 10 MINUTES WHAT YOU NEED

The Samsung phone you own The notification sound on your Galaxy phone can be easily changed if you prefer a different sound or just want to personalise your phone. The good news is that the procedures are identical whether you're using a high-end model like the Galaxy S23 Ultra or a more affordable one like the Galaxy S21 FA. If you own a Galaxy device, you can change the notification sound by following the instructions below.

HOW TO CHANGE ALL YOUR NOTIFICATIONS TO A NEW SOUND

When it comes to customizing alert tones, you have a few choices. The simplest solution is to make them all sound the same. If you do this, the sound of a text message will sound identical to that of an email. If you don't want to change the default sounds on your Galaxy device but don't need app-specific customization, this is the choice to choose. First Step: To access your quick settings on your Samsung phone, swipe down from the home screen.

Number Two: Go to the Preferences Menu (the Cogwheel).

CONNECTED • Top sales on the Samsung Galaxy S23 Ultra: Ways to obtain the phone at no cost Methods for deactivating a Google Smart Lock account Instructions for switching SIM cards between an Android phone and an iPhone 15

Third Step: Go to the Settings menu and choose the Sounds and Vibration option.

In the following menu, choose "Notification Sounds" as Step 4.

Here you may find a variety of notification sounds that you have the option to customize. If you choose this sound, it will be applied to all of your notifications.

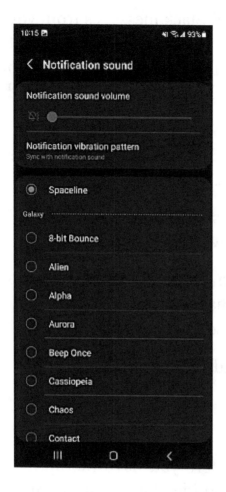

HOW TO SET A CUSTOMIZED NOTIFICATION FOR AN INDIVIDUAL APP

Although generic notification sounds should suffice, it may be helpful to have distinct notification sounds for each app if you frequently receive alerts from several sources, such as personal WhatsApp messages and Slack messages from your work team. If you're not a fan of the app's default sound, you may customize the notifications for each app separately to hear what you like. Take this step.

First thing to do: Swiping down again will bring up your Quick Settings menu; from there, click the Settings icon.

The second step is to find Apps and click on it once you scroll down.

Thirdly, the programs you've downloaded will be shown alphabetically. Choose the app whose notification sound you wish to modify.

Step 4: Find the Notifications option in the App's settings.

Fifth Step: Here you have the option to enable or disable app notifications. You can restrict the ability of specific apps on your Samsung phone to play sounds in this way. You should enable notifications if you want this app to make noise. Choose the categories for notifications in the page's footer.

Choose Miscellaneous from the Notification Categories dropdown in Step 6.

Sound. When you do this, the choice of possible notification sounds will appear once again, and you may select the one you like.

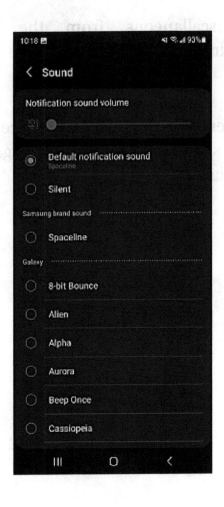

HOW TO CUSTOMIZE A SAMSUNG PHONE NOTIFICATION SOUNDS SOUND S23 HOW TO ADD NEW NOTIFICATION SOUNDS TO YOUR SAMSUNG PHONE

The default noises on Galaxy phones aren't to everyone's taste, but you can really install your own. Give it a try:

First things first: get the audio file you wish to utilize as the notification sound. Sending yourself an email with the desired audio clip and then accessing it on your phone is the simplest way to accomplish this. Find the download icon—an arrow heading downwards towards a straight line—in the audio attachment window and click on it.

Once you have your audio file downloaded, locate it in the My Files app by selecting Downloads. Due to your recent download, the file should now be displayed at the top of the downloads list.

Second, locate the audio file you just downloaded; then, at the screen's bottom, choose Move.

Step 3: Return to the main screen of My File and choose Internal storage after you have picked the file to move.

Fourth, change the drop-down choice inside the Internal storage menu to read All rather than Essentials. After you do that, a list of your device's available file storage locations will appear. Make your way to the Notifications folder.

Fifth, to move the file, go to the Notifications folder and, in the lower right corner, click the Move Here button.

When you're ready to add your own notification sounds, step six is to go to the settings and repeat the process from step five. With the addition of a new section called "Custom," your personalized notification sound will now be available when choosing the sound.

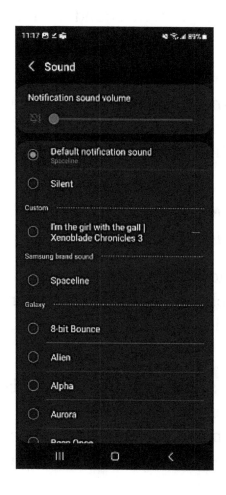

HOW TO REMOVE CUSTOM
NOTIFICATIONS ON A SAMSUNG PHONE

Are you sick of Samsung's new personalized notifications? Rest assured, they can be easily removed. Actually, the process of changing a notification sound to a custom sound and then uninstalling it is same.

To replace the custom sound with your device's default sound, follow the procedures outlined above for custom notification sounds, but instead of setting the custom sound in the sound menu, pick Default.

HOW TO SNOOZE NOTIFICATION SOUNDS ON A SAMSUNG PHONE

You may "snooze" notifications from individual apps on Galaxy smartphones if you're overwhelmed with notifications and would like to temporarily disable them.

1. Grab the gear symbol in the upper right corner of your screen or swipe down from the top of the screen to open the Quick Settings menu. From there, you can access all your device settings.
2. Find Notifications in the settings.
3. Go to the Notifications menu and choose Advanced Settings.
4. Enable the Show snooze button setting in the Advanced settings menu.
5. After you've enabled this feature, choose a notification from the app you wish to snooze.

Then, locate the bell icon in the notification's bottom left corner and click on it. Then, choose the amount of time you wish to ignore the alert. After you've made your selection, hit the Save button, and the app will stop sending you alerts for as long as you specified.

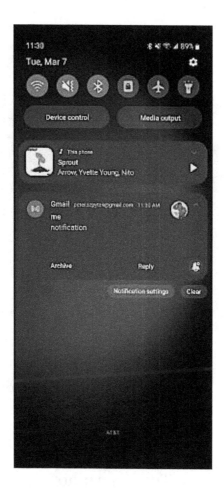

CHAPTER EIGHT

DOES THE SAMSUNG GALAXY S24 ULTRA HAVE A CURVED SCREEN?

Among Samsung's latest smartphone models, the Galaxy S24 Ultra stands head and shoulders above the others. Among its many impressive features, the smartphone has an upgraded camera system with a 200-megapixel primary sensor and a 50-megapixel 5x telephoto lens. The smartphone's screen is 40%

brighter than the previous-gen Galaxy S23 Ultra's. The new phone is also the first to ever be made of titanium.

IS THE GALAXY S24 ULTRA EQUIPPED WITH A CURVED SCREEN?

Would the Galaxy S24 Ultra keep the curved screen from previous iterations in terms of design and display? That very thing has been shown to us.

Is the S24 Ultra equipped with a curved screen, according to Samsung?

Screen from Samsung's Galaxy S24 Ultra.

Prakhar Khanna / Online Media Trends

As one of its most noticeable upgrades, the Galaxy S24 Ultra ditches the curved display for a flat one. Previous Galaxy S models, including the S23 Ultra, S22 Ultra, and S21 Ultra, had curved screens; this departs from that. Many Galaxy S fans are ecstatic that a flat-screen version is now available.

Related

Details regarding the Samsung Galaxy Z Fold 6, including when it will be released and how much it will cost

• The lowest prices on unlocked Samsung Galaxy S22 smartphones!

The fifteen best cases for the Samsung Galaxy S24 Ultra in 2024 are these.

The supposed immersive benefits of curved screens aren't worth the serious back ache they cause. The S24 Ultra's flat screen offers a great viewing experience without the issues that come with curved screens.

The Galaxy S24 Ultra's 6.8-inch QHD+ AMOLED screen boasts a 120Hz refresh rate. As a result, the screen's responsiveness and smoothness are both enhanced by the 120 Hz refresh rate. The screen is brighter than previous models, making it simpler to operate in harsh sunlight. The screen is protected by a newer version of Gorilla Glass that is more resistant to scratches and glare.

WHAT ABOUT THE GALAXY S24 AND S24 PLUS?

Furthermore, both the Galaxy S24 and the Galaxy S24 Plus feature flat panels. The 6.2-inch AMOLED screen of the Galaxy S24 has a Full HD+ resolution of 2340 x 1080 pixels and a refresh rate of 120 Hz. The 6.7-inch QHD+ screen of the Galaxy S24 Plus features an adjustable refresh rate of 120 Hz and a resolution of 3088 x 1440 pixels.

With options for 256GB, 512GB, or 1TB of storage, the Samsung Galaxy S24 Ultra is available in seven hues, including Titanium Orange and Titanium Gray. With features like Circle to Search, Live Translate, Interpreter, and more, all three of the new Galaxy S24 models come with sophisticated Galaxy AI capabilities.

CHAPTER TEN

TIPS AND TRICKS

One UI is one of the most feature-rich versions of Android thanks to Samsung's annual feature additions. Including the Galaxy S24 series, these updates are preloaded on all new Samsung phones.

If you're prepared to put in the work, you can find hidden riches everywhere. If you're using an older Galaxy S model (S23 or S22) and you're on Android 14, you can still use a lot of these, so don't be afraid to give them a try. Keep reading or watch the video up there, because we're going to talk about some fantastic features that you may test out.

Create An AI Wall Paper First.

Galaxy software from Samsung, like Pixel software from Google, has a feature that can make new wallpapers with just a few commands. Select Wallpaper and Style from the Settings menu to personalize your background. A "Creative" option will pop up. Once you've done so, proceed to the following screen and select the Generative folder.

After you choose a style, a screen will appear where you can produce visuals according to different commands by tapping the bold sentences. When you hit the "produce" button, a menu with four options will pop up. Tap Set to choose, or change the commands to make a new selection.

2. Coordinate The Wallpaper's Color Scheme With The Accent Colors Of Your Phone.

Even though Samsung's One UI doesn't automatically match wallpaper colors, you can change that setting. Select Wallpaper and Style from the Settings menu. Next, choose Color Palette. The Color Palette button has a toggle switch on its right side. Just power it on and select a few colors from the preset list that you prefer for your wallpaper.

My Experience with the Galaxy S24 Ultra

Using the Galaxy S24 Ultra for two weeks was both an impressive and tedious experience.

A third step is to get the translator app.

Thanks to a new interpretation app, users of Samsung phones may now converse with others who speak languages other than their own. To access Interpreter Mode, launch the app and then swipe down the Quick Settings menu. Next, choose the languages you would like to be able to speak.

This is by no means an exhaustive list, but it does cover the most common tongues. As soon as your finger touches the microphone to start speaking, it will immediately start transcribing your speech into text, translating it, and reading it aloud in the language you choose.

4. AI Notes From The Galaxy

A wealth of amazing features powered by AI become accessible the moment you enter 200 words or more into Notes. To open a note, just tap its star icon. Pick out the text you want to change, and then then choose Auto-Format with headings and bullet points, or as meeting notes. While Correct spelling does exactly what it says it would do—offers ideas for correcting typos—Summarize provides a brief, bulleted overview of the note's contents. well done

5 Double-Click To Identify Songs.

Many different functions can be given to the side key on Samsung devices. The ability to launch an app with a double-press is one example. If you install Shazam, click to its Settings, and enable the Shazam on startup option, the music detection software will detect music anytime it is opened. This way, you'll never have to hit that huge S button again.

Then, go to the Settings menu, then choose Advanced Features, and finally, choose Side Button. Click and drag After that, hit the "Open App" button after double-pressing on. Use the drop-down option to select Shazam. Now that you've set Shazam to launch automatically, when you double-press the side button, the app will start identifying the song.

6. Hit The Power Button Once More.

Pressing and holding the Side Button opens the Samsung assistant Bixby by default. Another option is to go to Settings > Advanced Features and Side Button to access the power menu through the side button. Seek out the "Power off" choice inside the "Press and Hold" submenu.

Pressing the lock screen clock will shorten the time.

Touching the clock on a Samsung lock screen opens a myriad of card widgets for various useful apps, like a voice recorder, music, weather, routines, and more. Within the Settings menu, you'll find the Lock Screen and AOD areas, where you can locate widgets. By selecting the reorder button at the top of the screen, you can rearrange the widgets in the desired sequence after you've selected them to display on the following screen.

8. Set Your Camera To Automatically Flash When A Notification Is Received.

More and more, you may configure your screen or camera to flash an LED light whenever new notifications come in. The flash notification option may be found in the Advanced Settings menu under the Accessibility section of the Settings menu. A toggle for the camera flash notification and the screen flash will show on the following screen when you touch it. The first one flashes your LED, while the second one lights up your screen.

9. Find Unread Notifications

Go to Settings > Notifications > Advanced Settings to see the Notification history option. If you touch it, a list of all the notifications that have been received to your phone can be displayed in categories. Simply scroll down to view all of the notifications that have been sent to your mobile device.

10.   Make The Battery Last Longer.

When you go to the Settings menu and look for Battery Protection, you should see three options. Make sure to enable Protection from the main menu before choosing a charging optimization. Always charge your battery to 80% capacity to prolong its life.

11. You Can Easily Screenshot By Swiping Left Or Right.

To take a screenshot on a Samsung phone, just slide your hand across the screen. Having this knowledge is useful for times when you would rather not use the side buttons. So long as it isn't already enabled, go to Settings > Advanced Features > Motions & Gestures to make it so. No, it has to be. You have the ability to toggle the capture function by swiping your palm.

12. The Screen Can Be Divided By Swiping Left Or Right.

the Advanced Features section of the Settings menu. By enabling it, you'll be able to swipe up with two fingers to switch between two apps simultaneously. The split-screen view describes this.

13. The Samsung Pop-Up Message

under the same heading as Advanced Features. Once turned on, swiping down from the corner will open any full-screen program in a floating window.

When you're in that view, you can drag it to move it across the screen using the tab at the top. A different option is to drag the tab to fill half of the screen to enter split-screen mode. When you tap that top bar once, a menu will display with options to fill the screen, change the transparency, minimize, or close the program.

14. Get Rid Of Samsung's Swipe-Up App

Many Samsung phone users have voiced their displeasure over the fact that, upon swiping up, the Samsung Pay function activates rather than recent apps or houses. Stopping it couldn't be easier, so that's good news. Once you've logged in and configured your Samsung Wallet, launch the app and press Menu at the bottom to access the app settings. Then, go to the upper right and you should see a gear icon. Once you've touched Quick Access, slide up to access it. You may disable it from the Home Screen, the Lock Screen, or even when the screen is off.

15. Use The Smartphone's Built-In Camera To Start Shooting.

The S Pen is capable of triggering a myriad of specific functions when coupled with the S24 Ultra. Holding down the pen's button will activate the camera. Once you've installed the camera app, taking images from a distance is as easy as pressing a button, and you can switch between the front and back cameras with just a double tap.

In addition, it comes with its own set of controls; for instance, to zoom in, hold down the button and make a clockwise circle motion; to zoom out, do the opposite. You can also swipe left or right to switch between the camera modes. Once you secure your phone to a tripod, you may film without touching the screen.

16. Using The Camera's Volume Controls

The volume buttons in the camera app are set to take pictures or start recording videos by default. However, zooming in is an option available to you. Launch the camera, locate the gear icon in the top right, and then choose settings to enter the shooting methods menu. Use the up-top volume controls to pinch-and-zoom.

17. A Fully Functional Gallery With Galaxy Ai

Several new AI features have been added to the Gallery app. Using one of these tools, you can move or delete subjects and objects from the scene.

Launch your preferred editor, open an existing photo, and then tap the pencil to access the editing page. Lastly, tap the blue star icon to save your changes. Tap and hold or draw a rectangle around an object to choose it. Simply slide it around or use the arrows on the corners to change its size. The eraser is still another tool at your disposal. Click the "generate" button when you're finished.

18.Slide And Drop To Edit Photos.

More so, if you open a picture in the gallery app and notice that anything specific is in the forefront, you can easily remove it from the snap by tapping and holding on it. When you're done, you can either copy and paste it into a document, share it, or put it on your Samsung Keyboard as a sticker.

19.Install A Galati Landscape By Reorienting Your Home Screen.

Although you might prefer the Home Screen in landscape orientation on bigger screens, it does not automatically switch to that manner. To access the Settings menu, press and hold the background image. Grab hold of the "Turn to landscape" icon.

20. Galaxy Ai Website Summary

Find the article you want to summarize on Samsung Internet. A quick tap on the AI star icon in the toolbar will bring up Summarize. Next, it will read the entire page and then provide you a brief summary of the article's key points in bullet points.

21. Searching On Google

To take a screenshot that Google's sophisticated picture recognition algorithm can examine, just draw a circle around an object in the image and then tap and hold the bottom border of the screen. The application will then display the object's data, such as its name, price, and, in certain cases, a link to purchase it.

22.   Galaxy AI Text Tone Detectors

The latest AI feature in Samsung Keyboard allows it to identify and change the tone of each text message. Simply press the star-shaped button on the toolbar after you begin typing to activate AI. A wider range of tones will be generated when you select Writing Style from the drop-down menu, including formal, informal, emoji-feed, and social media-ready.

www.ingramcontent.com/pod-product-compliance
Lightning Source LLC
Chambersburg PA
CBHW071253050326
40690CB00011B/2380